ONE-POT PASTA

FROM POT
TO PLATE
*in under 30
minutes*

SABRINA FAUDA-RÔLE
PHOTOGRAPHY BY AKIKO IDA

hardie grant books

CONTENTS

THE BASICS 4

MEAT PASTA

Meatballs in tomato sauce.. 6

Carbonara 8

Pancetta and sun-dried tomatoes.................................. 10

Smoked ham and pumpkin.. 12

Artichoke and lardons.. 14

Ham and Gruyère.. 16

Porcini and lardons.. 18

Asparagus and bacon 20

Swiss chard and smoked streaky bacon 22

Smoked sausage.. 24

Chorizo and sweetcorn 26

Roast chicken and mushrooms...................................... 28

Chicken, pistachios and ricotta..................................... 30

Turkey and peas.. 32

Veal with paprika... 34

FISH PASTA

Tuna, capers and Parmesan.. 36

Tuna, courgettes and mint... 38

Smoked mackerel and leeks.. 40

Spinach and smoked salmon.. 42

Courgettes and prawns 44

Anchovies, olives and tomatoes.................................... 46

Mixed seafood... 48

Thai salmon... 50

VEGGIE PASTA

Tomato and basil 52

Quick pesto 54

Carrots, curry and sesame 56

Aubergines and tomatoes 58

Orechiette primavera... 60

Winter vegetables... 62

CHEESE PASTA

Gorgonzola and mushrooms... 64

Goat's cheese, tomatoes and olives.............................. 66

Roquefort and courgettes.. 68

Four cheeses... 70

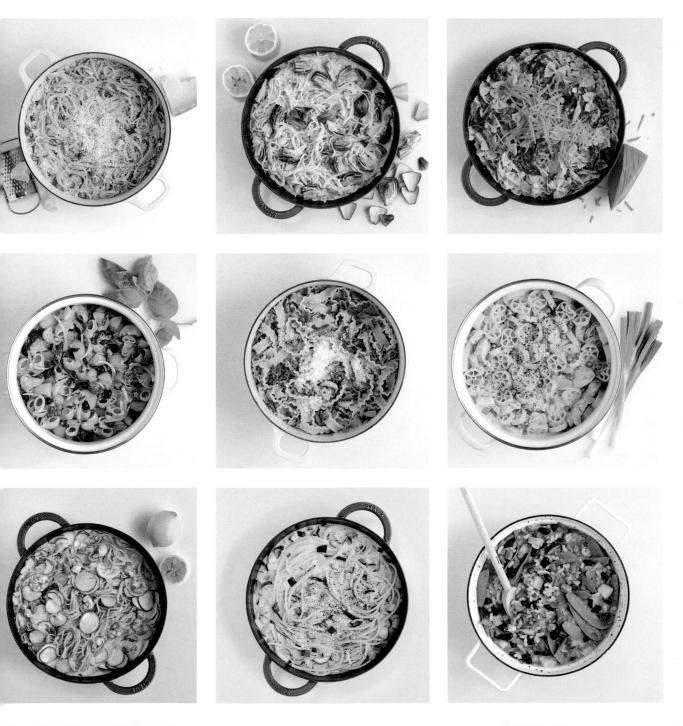

THE BASICS

THE CONCEPT

All the ingredients for the pasta dish are cooked together and simmered in a small amount of water at the same time. The starch released by the pasta during cooking, along with all the other ingredients, creates a delicious creamy sauce, making a pasta dish in record time using just one pot.

THE STAGES

1. Put the pasta into a large saucepan or casserole dish (24 cm/8 in minimum, 28 cm/12 in for long pasta).

2. Add all the other ingredients.

3. Pour in the water and stir.

4. Place over a medium heat and cook for around 15 minutes, stirring regularly. Around 2 cm (¾ in) of liquid should remain at the bottom of the pan at the end of cooking.

5. Remove from the heat and leave to stand for 5 minutes, stirring regularly: the pasta will finish cooking without sticking and the sauce will thicken to the right consistency. If you serve it straight away, the pasta will not be fully cooked and the sauce will be too runny.

6. Serve with any garnish suggested. The dishes are already seasoned with salt and pepper, but do taste the food and adjust if necessary before serving.

THE PASTA

Choose good-quality dried pasta, which will remain intact when cooked. Do not use quick-cooking pasta. You can switch various types of pasta as long as they have the same cooking time.

CREAMY INGREDIENTS

These can be added at the beginning of the cooking time to give body and a creamy consistency to the sauce (double/heavy cream, mascarpone, butter, olive oil). You can also use products that are already cooked (tomato sauce, baba ganoush, cheese with garlic and herbs etc.).

FLAVOURS AND SEASONINGS

Enhance flavour with onions, shallots, garlic, aromatic herbs, stock cubes etc.

SPICES AND CONDIMENTS

Boost the flavour further and add a distinctive twist with basil, chives, chilli, lemon zest etc.

HIGHLY FLAVOURED INGREDIENTS

Use ingredients with strong flavours to add character to the pasta. They will give the dish its dominant flavour (smoked fish, lardons, smoked ham, Roquefort etc.).

CRUNCHY INGREDIENTS

Where possible, use organic vegetables. You can use frozen produce (meatballs, cooked mushrooms etc.), as it will defrost during cooking. Avoid tinned vegetables, as they tend to disintegrate. You can also add an extra crunch by including ingredients such as walnuts, pistachios or pine kernels.

WATER

Always use cold water; with hot water the pasta will soften much too quickly. Use precise quantities otherwise your pasta will be undercooked or overcooked.

GARNISHES

For a final touch, add Parmesan or other grated cheese, chopped fresh herbs, rocket (arugula) or pepper.

MEATBALLS IN TOMATO SAUCE

SERVES 4 / 15 MINS

INGREDIENTS

250 g (9 oz) spaghetti
12 pre-cooked meatballs
350 g (12 oz) passata
1 onion, thinly sliced
2 garlic cloves, thinly sliced
2 tablespoons olive oil
4 sprigs of thyme
8 large basil leaves
2 bay leaves
1 teaspoon rock salt
freshly ground black pepper
750 ml (25 fl oz) water
grated Parmesan, to serve
handful of rocket (arugula), to serve

METHOD

Put all the ingredients into a large saucepan in the order listed. Cook for approximately 15 minutes over a medium heat, stirring regularly. About 2 cm (¾ in) of cooking liquid should remain at the end. Serve with grated Parmesan and rocket.

CARBONARA

SERVES 4 / 15 MINS

INGREDIENTS

250 g (9 oz) linguine
200 g (7 oz) smoked lardons
1 onion, thinly sliced
2 eggs
½ bunch of chives, snipped
4 tablespoons grated Parmesan
  + a little more to serve
1 teaspoon rock salt
4 tablespoons olive oil
freshly ground black pepper
750 ml (25 fl oz) water

METHOD

Put all the ingredients into a large saucepan in the order listed. Cook for approximately 15 minutes over a medium heat, stirring regularly. About 2 cm (¾ in) of cooking liquid should remain at the end. Serve with grated Parmesan.

PANCETTA AND SUN-DRIED TOMATOE

SERVES 4 / 15 MINS

INGREDIENTS

250 g (9 oz) whole-wheat fusilli
250 g (9 oz) mozzarella
140 g (5 oz) sun-dried tomatoes
   marinated in oil + their oil
100 g (3½ oz) sliced pancetta
2 teaspoons oregano
1 onion, thinly sliced

1 vegetable stock cube
8 basil leaves
freshly ground black pepper
750 ml (25 fl oz) water
2 handfuls of rocket (arugula) leaves

METHOD

Put all the other ingredients, except the rocket, into a large saucepan in the order listed. Cook for approximately 15 minutes over a medium heat, stirring. About 2 cm (¾ in) of cooking liquid should remain at the end. Stir in the rocket.

SMOKED HAM AND PUMPKIN

SERVES 4 / 15 MINS

INGREDIENTS

250 g (9 oz) penne
200 g (7 oz) smoked cured
   ham, thinly sliced
500 g (1 lb 2 oz) pumpkin (squash),
   peeled and diced
12 sage leaves
2 large shallots, thinly sliced
25 g (¾ oz) butter
2 pinches of nutmeg
2 sprigs of rosemary
1 teaspoon rock salt
freshly ground black pepper
750 ml (25 fl oz) water

METHOD

Put all the ingredients into a
large saucepan in the order
listed. Cook for approximately
15 minutes over a medium
heat, stirring regularly.
About 2 cm (¾ in) of cooking
liquid should remain at the end.

ARTICHOKE AND LARDONS

SERVES 4 / 15 MINS

INGREDIENTS

250 g (9 oz) vermicelli
4 fresh artichoke hearts or 250 g
　(9 oz) frozen artichoke, quartered
100 g (3½ oz) smoked lardons
1 onion, thinly sliced
1 garlic clove, finely chopped
125 g (4 oz) mascarpone

2 tablespoons grated pecorino
juice of 1 lemon
2 tablespoons olive oil
1 teaspoon rock salt
freshly ground black pepper
750 ml (25 fl oz) water

METHOD

Put all the ingredients into a large saucepan in the order listed. Cook for approximately 15 minutes over a medium heat, stirring regularly. About 2 cm (¾ in) of cooking liquid should remain at the end.

HAM AND GRUYÈRE

SERVES 4 / 15 MINS

INGREDIENTS

250 g (9 oz) macaroni
180 g (6 oz) slices of cooked
  ham, torn into pieces
150 g (5 oz) frozen peas
150 g (5 oz) soft cheese
40 g (1½ oz) sautéed onions
1 vegetable stock cube
1 small bunch of chives, snipped
2 tablespoons olive oil
freshly ground black pepper
750 ml (25 fl oz) water
grated Gruyère, to serve

METHOD

Set aside a small amount of the snipped chives. Put all the other ingredients into a large saucepan in the order listed. Cook for approximately 15 minutes over a medium heat, stirring regularly. About 2 cm (¾ in) of cooking liquid should remain at the end. Serve with the grated cheese and reserved chives.

PORCINI AND LARDONS

SERVES 4 / 15 MINS

INGREDIENTS

250 g (9 oz) Mafaldine or Reginette
100 g (3½ oz) dried porcini
    mushrooms
200 g (7 oz) button
    mushrooms, thinly sliced
100 g (3½ oz) smoked lardons
2 shallots, thinly sliced
1 garlic clove, thinly sliced
1 sprig of thyme

1 sprig of rosemary
200 ml (7 fl oz) double
    (heavy) cream
2 tablespoons grated Parmesan
    + a little to serve
freshly ground black pepper
1 teaspoon rock salt
750 ml (25 fl oz) water

METHOD

Put all the ingredients into a large
saucepan in the order listed. Cook
for approximately 15 minutes over
a medium heat, stirring regularly.
About 2 cm (¾ in) of cooking
liquid should remain at the end.
Serve with grated Parmesan.

ASPARAGUS AND BACON

SERVES 4 / 15 MINS

INGREDIENTS

250 g (9 oz) penne
250 g (9 oz) asparagus spears,
    sliced into 3 cm (1 in) sections
100 g (3½ oz) lardons
250 g (9 oz) soft cheese
    with garlic and herbs
1 onion, thinly sliced
2 tablespoons olive oil
1 teaspoon rock salt
freshly ground black pepper
750 ml (25 fl oz) water

METHOD

Put all the ingredients into a
large saucepan in the order
listed. Cook for approximately
15 minutes over a medium
heat, stirring regularly. About
2 cm (¾ in) of cooking liquid
should remain at the end.

SWISS CHARD AND SMOKED STREAKY BACON

SERVES 4 / 15 MINS

INGREDIENTS

250 g (9 oz) whole-wheat penne
250 g (9 oz) Swiss chard
   leaves, coarsely chopped
100 g (3½ oz) smoked streaky bacon
200 g (7 oz) tinned
   chopped tomatoes
1 onion, thinly sliced

2 garlic cloves, thinly sliced
1 vegetable stock cube
4 sprigs of thyme
2 bay leaves
freshly ground black pepper
650 ml (21 fl oz) water

METHOD

Put all the ingredients into a large saucepan in the order listed. Cook for approximately 15 minutes over a medium heat, stirring regularly. About 2 cm (¾ in) of cooking liquid should remain at the end.

SMOKED SAUSAGE

SERVES 4 / 15 MINS

INGREDIENTS

250 g (9 oz) fusilli
250 g (9 oz) smoked sausage
200 g (7 oz) passata
250 g (9 oz) frozen mixed mushrooms
1 small bunch of parsley, finely chopped
1 onion, thinly sliced
2 garlic cloves, thinly sliced
1 teaspoon rock salt
freshly ground black pepper
750 ml (25 fl oz) water

METHOD

Set aside 1 tablespoon of chopped parsley. Put all the other ingredients into a large saucepan in the order listed. Cook for approximately 15 minutes over a medium heat, stirring regularly. About 2 cm (¾ in) of cooking liquid should remain at the end. Sprinkle the parsley on top.

CHORIZO AND SWEETCORN

SERVES 4 / 15 MINS

INGREDIENTS

250 g (9 oz) farfalle
6 mini red, green and yellow
   peppers, thinly sliced
90 g (3 oz) chorizo, cut into thin slices
340 g (12 oz) tinned sweetcorn,
   drained and rinsed
4 small tomatoes, quartered
1 onion, thinly sliced
1 pinch of Cayenne pepper
1 small sprig of coriander (cilantro)
2 tablespoons olive oil
1 teaspoon rock salt
freshly ground black pepper
750 ml (25 fl oz) water
grated Cheddar, to serve

METHOD

Put all the ingredients into a
large saucepan in the order
listed. Cook for approximately
15 minutes, stirring regularly.
About 2 cm (¾ in) of cooking
liquid should remain at the end.
Serve with the grated Cheddar.

ROAST CHICKEN AND MUSHROOMS

SERVES 4 / 15 MIN

INGREDIENTS

250 g (9 oz) farfalle
300 g (10½ oz) roast chicken
  leftovers + meat juices
250 g (9 oz) mixed frozen
  cooked mushrooms
1 onion, thinly sliced

250 ml (9 fl oz) double
  (heavy) cream
1 teaspoon coarse salt
freshly ground black pepper
750 ml (25 fl oz) water

METHOD

Put all the ingredients into a large saucepan in the order listed. Cook for approximately 15 minutes over a medium heat, stirring regularly. About 2 cm (¾ in) of cooking liquid should remain at the end.

CHICKEN, PISTACHIOS AND RICOTTA

SERVES 4 / 15 MINS

INGREDIENTS

250 g (9 oz) gnocchi
6 chicken breasts, shredded
250 g (9 oz) ricotta
50 g (2 oz) pine kernels
50 g (2 oz) hulled pistachios
2 large shallots, thinly sliced
1 garlic clove, thinly sliced
1 vegetable stock cube
2 sprigs of rosemary
1 teaspoon ground aniseed
2 tablespoons olive oil
freshly ground black pepper
750 ml (25 fl oz) water
4 sprigs of coriander (cilantro)

METHOD

Set aside half of the ricotta and the coriander. Put all the other ingredients into a large saucepan in the order listed. Cook for approximately 15 minutes over a medium heat, stirring regularly. About 2 cm (¾ in) of cooking liquid should remain at the end. Serve with the coriander and the remaining ricotta.

TURKEY AND PEAS

SERVES 4 / 15 MINS

INGREDIENTS

250 g (9 oz) rotelle
250 g (9 oz) turkey fillets
250 g (9 oz) frozen peas
1 Saint-Marcellin or other soft,
    creamy cheese, cut into chunks
4 leeks or 2 spring onions
    (scallions), thinly sliced

1 garlic clove, thinly sliced
1 chicken stock cube
200 ml (7 fl oz) single (light) cream
freshly ground black pepper
750 ml (25 fl oz) water

METHOD

Put all the ingredients into a large
saucepan in the order listed. Cook
for approximately 15 minutes over
a medium heat, stirring regularly.
About 2 cm (¾ in) of cooking
liquid should remain at the end.

VEAL WITH PAPRIKA

SERVES 4 / 15 MINS

INGREDIENTS

250 g (9 oz) rigatoni
350 g (12 oz) veal mince
4 small tomatoes, quartered
1 small bunch of tarragon,
   stalks removed
1 tablespoon paprika
150 g (5 oz) passata

1 onion, thinly sliced
2 garlic cloves, thinly sliced
2 tablespoons olive oil
1 teaspoon rock salt
freshly ground black pepper
750 ml (25 fl oz) water

METHOD

Put all the ingredients into a large saucepan in the order listed. Cook for approximately 15 minutes over a medium heat, stirring regularly. About 2 cm (¾ in) of cooking liquid should remain at the end.

TUNA, CAPERS AND PARMESAN

SERVES 4 / 15 MINS

INGREDIENTS

350 g (12 oz) linguine
200 g (7 oz) tinned tuna in olive oil
80 g (3 oz) capers
12 basil leaves, snipped
100 g (3½ oz) grated Parmesan
  + a little to serve
zest and juice of 1 lemon

1 vegetable stock cube
1 onion, thinly sliced
2 garlic cloves, thinly sliced
4 tablespoons olive oil
freshly ground black pepper
900 ml (33 fl oz) water

METHOD

Put all the ingredients into a large saucepan in the order listed. Cook for approximately 15 minutes over a medium heat, stirring regularly. About 2 cm (¾ in) of cooking liquid should remain at the end. Serve with grated Parmesan.

TUNA, COURGETTES AND MINT

SERVES 4 / 15 MINS

INGREDIENTS

250 g (9 oz) penne
150 g (5 oz) tuna fillets in olive oil
2 courgettes (zucchini), cut
   into ribbons
1 small bunch of mint,
   stalks removed, 6 leaves snipped
1 tablespoon ground
   coriander (cilantro)

1 vegetable stock cube
1 onion, thinly sliced
1 shallot, thinly sliced
2 garlic cloves, thinly sliced
2 tablespoons olive oil
1 teaspoon rock salt
freshly ground black pepper
750 ml (25 fl oz) water

METHOD

Set aside the snipped mint leaves.
Put all the other ingredients into a
saucepan in the order listed. Cook
for approximately 15 minutes over
a medium heat, stirring regularly.
About 2 cm (¾ in) of cooking
liquid should remain at the end.
Sprinkle with the snipped mint.

SMOKED MACKEREL AND LEEKS

SERVES 4 / 15 MINS

INGREDIENTS

250 g (9 oz) eliche pasta (spirals)
1 peppered smoked mackerel
   fillet, skin removed
2 leeks, thinly sliced
1 shallot, thinly sliced
1 garlic clove, thinly sliced
10 g (½ oz) ginger, grated
200 ml (7 fl oz) double (heavy) cream
2 tablespoons olive oil
1 teaspoon rock salt
750 ml (25 fl oz) water

METHOD

Put all the ingredients into a large saucepan in the order listed. Cook for approximately 15 minutes over a medium heat, stirring regularly. About 2 cm (¾ in) of cooking liquid should remain at the end.

SPINACH AND SMOKED SALMON

SERVES 4 / 15 MINS

INGREDIENTS

350 g (12 oz) tagliatelle
125 g (4 oz) fresh spinach
160 g (5 oz) smoked salmon
2 large shallots, thinly sliced
2 garlic cloves, thinly sliced
4 tablespoons double (heavy) cream
1 vegetable stock cube
freshly ground black pepper
750 ml (25 fl oz) water

METHOD

Put all the ingredients into a large saucepan in the order listed. Cook for approximately 15 minutes over a medium heat, stirring regularly. About 2 cm (¾ in) of cooking liquid should remain at the end.

COURGETTES AND PRAWNS

SERVES 4 / 15 MINS

INGREDIENTS

250 g (9 oz) whole-wheat spaghetti
200 g (7 oz) shelled prawns (shrimp)
2 courgettes (zucchini),
    cut into thin rounds
250 g (9 oz) mascarpone
zest of 1 lemon
juice of ½ lemon

½ lemon, sliced
1 small bunch of dill
1 vegetable stock cube
2 tablespoons olive oil
1 teaspoon rock salt
freshly ground black pepper
750 ml (25 fl oz) water

METHOD

Put all the ingredients into a large saucepan in the order listed. Cook for approximately 15 minutes over a medium heat, stirring regularly. About 2 cm (¾ in) of cooking liquid should remain at the end.

ANCHOVIES, OLIVES AND TOMATOES

SERVES 4 / 15 MINS

INGREDIENTS

250 g (9 oz) gnocchetti
50 g (2 oz) anchovy fillets
4 small tomatoes, quartered
150 g (5 oz) green olives, pitted
10 basil leaves, torn
1 onion, thinly sliced
2 garlic cloves, thinly sliced

200 ml (7 fl oz) single (light) cream
2 tablespoons olive oil
freshly ground black pepper
750 ml (25 fl oz) water
grated Parmesan, to serve

METHOD

Put all the ingredients into a large saucepan in the order listed. Cook for approximately 15 minutes over a medium heat, stirring regularly. About 2 cm (¾ in) of cooking liquid should remain at the end. Serve with grated Parmesan.

MIXED SEAFOOD

SERVES 4 / 15 MINS

INGREDIENTS

250 g (9 oz) spaghetti
200 g (7 oz) frozen mussels
200 g (7 oz) frozen scallops
100 g (3½ oz) frozen shelled
  prawns (shrimp)
100 g (3½ oz) frozen peas
4 small tomatoes, quartered
200 g (7 oz) tinned tomatoes
1 onion, thinly sliced
1 garlic clove, thinly sliced
1 vegetable stock cube
1 pinch of saffron
1 small bunch of parsley
4 tablespoons olive oil
1 teaspoon rock salt
freshly ground black pepper
750 ml (25 fl oz) water

METHOD

Put all the ingredients into a large saucepan in the order listed. Cook for approximately 15 minutes over a medium heat, stirring regularly. About 2 cm (¾ in) of cooking liquid should remain at the end.

THAI SALMON

SERVES 4 / 15 MINS

INGREDIENTS

250 g (9 oz) capellini
2 salmon steaks, fresh or frozen
250 ml (8½ fl oz) coconut milk
4 small tomatoes, quartered
2 mini peppers, thinly sliced
1 small sprig of coriander (cilantro)
2 garlic cloves, thinly sliced
1 onion, thinly sliced
2 bay leaves
5 cm (2 in) lemongrass stalk, thinly sliced
10 g (½ oz) ginger, grated
zest and juice of 1 lime
1 vegetable stock cube
1 teaspoon sugar
1 tablespoon curry powder
1 teaspoon rock salt
freshly ground black pepper
750 ml (25 fl oz) water

METHOD

Set aside a few coriander leaves for garnish. Put all the other ingredients into a large saucepan in the order listed. Cook for approximately 15 minutes over a medium heat, stirring regularly. About 2 cm (¾ in) of cooking liquid should remain at the end. Sprinkle the remaining coriander leaves on top.

TOMATO AND BASIL

SERVES 4 / 15 MINS

INGREDIENTS

350 g (12 oz) linguine
250 g (9 oz) cherry tomatoes, halved
2 garlic cloves, thinly sliced
1 onion, thinly sliced
4 tablespoons olive oil
1 small red pepper, thinly sliced
4 sprigs of basil

1 tablespoon rock salt
freshly ground black pepper
900 ml (33 fl oz) water
grated Parmesan, to serve

METHOD

Put all the ingredients into a large saucepan in the order listed. Cook for approximately 15 minutes over a medium heat, stirring regularly. About 2 cm (¾ in) of cooking liquid should remain at the end. Serve with grated Parmesan.

QUICK PESTO

SERVES 4 / 15 MINS

INGREDIENTS

200 g (7 fl oz) pasta shells
2 garlic cloves, thinly sliced
2 courgettes (zucchini), diced
150 g (5 oz) French beans, tops
    removed, cut into
    1 cm (½ in) lengths
250 g (9 oz) tinned kidney
    beans, drained and rinsed
125 g (4 oz) mangetout (snow peas)
4 small tomatoes, diced
150 g (5 oz) green pesto
4 tablespoons olive oil
1 teaspoon rock salt
freshly ground black pepper
1 litre (34 fl oz) water
grated Parmesan, to serve

METHOD

Set aside half of the pesto
for garnish. Put all the other
ingredients into a large
saucepan in the order listed.
Cook for approximately
15 minutes over a medium
heat, stirring regularly. About
4 cm (1½ in) of cooking liquid
should remain at the end.
Add the remaining pesto and
serve with grated Parmesan.

CARROTS, CURRY AND SESAME

SERVES 4 / 15 MINS

INGREDIENTS

250 g (9 oz) whole-wheat spaghetti
1 carrot, grated
250 ml (8½ fl oz) coconut milk
1 small sprig of coriander (cilantro)
1 teaspoon curry powder
1 teaspoon sesame oil
20 g (¾ oz) golden sesame seeds
2 spring onions (scallions), thinly sliced
1 garlic clove, thinly sliced
1 teaspoon rock salt
750 ml (25 fl oz) water

METHOD

Set aside a few slices of spring onion and sesame seeds. Put all the other ingredients into a large saucepan in the order listed. Cook for approximately 15 minutes over a medium heat, stirring regularly. About 2 cm (¾ in) of cooking liquid should remain at the end. Sprinkle the remaining sliced spring onions and sesame seeds on top.

AUBERGINE AND TOMATOES

SERVES 4 / 15 MINS

INGREDIENTS

250 g (9 oz) pipe rigate
250 g (9 oz) baba ganoush
12 cherry tomatoes, halved
20 basil leaves, torn
1 onion, thinly sliced
2 garlic cloves, thinly sliced
2 sprigs of thyme
2 tablespoons olive oil
1 teaspoon rock salt
freshly ground black pepper
750 ml (25 fl oz) water
20 mini balls of mozzarella (150 g/5 oz)

METHOD

Set aside half the basil and the mozzarella. Put all the other ingredients into a large saucepan in the order listed. Cook for approximately 15 minutes over a medium heat, stirring regularly. About 2 cm (¾ in) of cooking liquid should remain at the end. Serve with the mozzarella melted into the pasta and the remaining basil.

ORECHIETTE PRIMAVERA

SERVES 4 / 15 MINS

INGREDIENTS

250 g (9 oz) orechiette
200 g (7 oz) broccoli, cut into florets
150 g (5 oz) frozen broad beans
150 g (5 oz) French beans,
    cut into 1 cm (½ in) lengths
2 garlic cloves, thinly sliced
1 onion, thinly sliced
juice and zest of 1 lemon

2 tablespoons olive oil
200 ml (7 fl oz) single (light) cream
1 vegetable stock cube
1 teaspoon rock salt
freshly ground black pepper
750 ml (25 fl oz) water
shaved Parmesan, to serve

METHOD

Put all the ingredients into a large saucepan in the order listed. Cook for approximately 15 minutes over a medium heat, stirring regularly. About 2 cm (¾ in) of cooking liquid should remain at the end. Serve with grated Parmesan.

WINTER VEGETABLES

SERVES 4 / 15 MINS

INGREDIENTS

250 g (9 oz) spaghetti, broken up
1 carrot, finely diced
1 leek, thinly sliced
1 turnip, finely diced
2 Jerusalem artichokes, finely diced
2 celery sticks, finely diced
1 vegetable stock cube
1 onion, thinly sliced
1 shallot, thinly sliced
2 garlic cloves, thinly sliced
2 sprigs of thyme
1 bay leaf
1 bunch of chives, snipped
25 g (¾ oz) butter
1 teaspoon rock salt
freshly ground black pepper
1 litre (34 fl oz) water
grated Gruyère, to serve

METHOD

Put all of the ingredients into a large saucepan in the order listed. Cook for approximately 15 minutes over a medium heat, stirring regularly. About 4 cm (1½ in) of cooking liquid should remain at the end. Serve with grated Gruyère.

GORGONZOLA AND MUSHROOMS

SERVES 4 / 15 MINS

INGREDIENTS

250 g (9 oz) pantacce
   (or mafalde corte)
200 g (7 oz) button
   mushrooms, quartered
100 g (3½ oz) mascarpone
200 g (7 oz) gorgonzola
100 g (3½ oz) chopped walnuts
1 shallot, thinly sliced

1 small bunch of parsley, chopped
1 teaspoon rock salt
freshly ground black pepper
750 ml (25 fl oz) water

METHOD

Set aside 1 teaspoon of parsley.
Put all of the ingredients into a
large saucepan in the order listed.
Cook for approximately 15 minutes
over a medium heat, stirring.
About 2 cm (¾ in) of cooking
liquid should remain at the end.
Sprinkle the parsley on top.

GOAT'S CHEESE, TOMATOES AND OLIVES

SERVES 4 / 15 MINS

INGREDIENTS

250 g (9 oz) pipe rigate
200 g (7 oz) cherry tomatoes, halved
150 g (5 oz) fresh goat's cheese
125 g (4 oz) black olives (Niçoise)
1 small bunch of basil, torn
1 garlic clove, thinly sliced
1 onion, thinly sliced
4 tablespoons olive oil
1 sprig of thyme
1 sprig of rosemary
freshly ground black pepper
1 teaspoon rock salt
750 ml (25 fl oz) water

METHOD

Put all the ingredients into a large saucepan in the order listed. Cook for approximately 15 minutes over a medium heat, stirring regularly. About 2 cm (¾ in) of cooking liquid should remain at the end.

ROQUEFORT AND COURGETTES

SERVES 4 / 15 MINS

INGREDIENTS

250 g (9 oz) bucatini
2 small courgettes (zucchini), diced
150 g (5 oz) Roquefort,
    cut into large chunks
1 garlic clove, thinly sliced
200 ml (7 fl oz) single (light) cream
1 onion, thinly sliced

1 small bunch of parsley
1 vegetable stock cube
2 tablespoons olive oil
freshly ground black pepper
1 teaspoon rock salt
750 ml (25 fl oz) water

METHOD

Put all the ingredients into a large saucepan in the order listed. Cook for approximately 15 minutes over a medium heat, stirring regularly. About 2 cm (¾ in) of cooking liquid should remain at the end.

FOUR CHEESES

SERVES 4 / 15 MINS

INGREDIENTS

250 g (9 oz) galletti
100 g (3½ oz) Fourme d'Ambert
60 g (2 oz) matured goat's cheese,
  crottin type (if available)
100 g (3½ oz) grated Comté
150 g (5 oz) mascarpone
1 garlic clove, thinly sliced
2 pinches of nutmeg

½ bunch of chives, snipped
1 sprig of thyme
1 sprig of rosemary
2 bay leaves
freshly ground black pepper
750 ml (25 fl oz) water

METHOD

Set aside a few chives. Put all
the other ingredients into a large
saucepan in the order listed.
Cook for approximately 15 minutes
over a medium heat, stirring regularly.
About 2 cm (¾ in) of cooking
liquid should remain at the end.
Sprinkle the snipped chives on top.

ACKNOWLEDGEMENTS

With thanks to Akiko, Rose-Marie and Pauline.
Thanks to Nina and Quentin for their patience.
And thanks to our guinea pigs: Charles, Sophie, Roch, Ivan, Charlotte, Lili.

One-Pot Pasta by Sabrina Fauda-Rôle

First published in 2015 by Hachette Books (Marabout)
This English hardback edition published in 2016 by Hardie Grant Books

Hardie Grant Books (UK)
52–54 Southwark Street
London SE1 1UN
hardiegrant.co.uk

Hardie Grant Books (Australia)
Ground Floor, Building 1
658 Church Street
Melbourne, VIC 3121
hardiegrant.com.au

The moral rights of Sabrina Fauda-Rôle to be identified as the author
of this work have been asserted by her in accordance with the
Copyright, Designs and Patents Act 1988.

British Library Cataloguing-in-Publication Data. A catalogue record
for this book is available from the British Library.

ISBN: 978-1-78488-057-6

Photographer: Akiko Ida
Design: Frédéric Voisin
Proofreading: Audrey Genin and Véronique Dussidour

For the English hardback edition:
Publisher: Kate Pollard
Senior Editor: Kajal Mistry
Editorial Assistant: Hannah Roberts
Editor: Nicky Lovick
Translation: Gilla Evans
Colour Reproduction by p2d

Printed and bound in China by 1010

10 9 8 7 6 5 4 3 2 1